DIVING AND SNORKELING GUIDE TO

The Bahamas
Nassau and
New Providence Island
Second Edition

DIVING AND SNORKELING GUIDE TO

The Bahamas
Nassau and
New Providence Island
Second Edition

Steve Blount and Lisa Walker

Pisces Books
A Division of Gulf Publishing Company
Houston, Texas

Library of Congress Cataloging-in-Publication Data
Blount, Steve.
     Diving and snorkeling guide to the Bahamas: Nassau and
 New Providence Island/by Steve Blount and Lisa
 Walker—2nd ed.
     p. cm.
 Includes index.
 ISBN 1-55992-040-8
     1. Skin diving—Bahamas. 2. Bahamas—Description and
 travel—1981—Guide-books. 3. Skin diving—Bahamas—
 Nassau—Guide-books. 4. Skin diving—Bahamas—New
 Providence Island—Guide-books. I. Walker, Lisa. II. Pisces
 Books (Firm) III. Title.
 GV840.S78B53 1990
 797.2′3′097296—dc20   90-43484
                                                          CIP

Printed in Hungary

Acknowledgments

The authors would especially like to thank Stuart Cove, Roscoe Knowles, and John Pierre "Doc" Genasi of Nassau Undersea Adventures for their assistance in compiling and revising this guide. They shared generously of their knowledge of Nassau and its marine environment. Others whose contributions can't be ignored include Greg Lee of Bahamian News Service, Ltd., and Steve Sweeting and Lambert Albury of Sun Divers. Thanks also are due to Woodrow Wilson of Bahamasair, Carl Minns of the Bahamas Ministry of Tourism, and the staff of the Bahamas Ministry of Tourism office in Coral Gables, Florida.

Table of Contents

How To Use This Guide

New Providence Island, one of the first stops for Spanish explorers in the New World, is now a new world for divers. This guide can help you discover that new world. In Chapter 1, you'll find an overview of New Providence and Nassau, along with information on how to get there, customs and immigration rules, shopping, sightseeing, and dining. Chapter 2 surveys the diving areas around the island and the diving operators. Chapter 3 gives detailed descriptions and photos of a variety of dive sites.

Much of the shallow ocean area surrounding New Providence has been designated a marine park by the Bahamian government. No spearfishing is allowed within the park boundaries, and the taking of live shells, corals, or other living creatures is forbidden. The marine park area is outlined on the map on page 33.

New Providence has an almost magnetic attraction for film directors. This steel wreck was deliberately sunk as a prop for the movie Never Say Never Again. ◊

The Rating System for Divers and Dives

Our suggestions as to the minimum level of expertise required for any given dive should be taken in a conservative sense, keeping in mind the old adage about there being old divers and bold divers, but few old, bold divers. We consider a *novice* to be someone in decent physical condition, who has recently completed a basic certification diving course, or a certified diver who has not been been diving recently or who has no experience in similar waters. We consider an *intermediate* diver to be a certified diver in excellent physical condition who has been diving actively for at least one year following a basic course, and who has been diving recently in similar waters. We consider an *advanced* diver to be someone who has completed an advanced certification course, has been diving recently in similar waters, and is in excellent physical condition. You will have to decide if you are capable of making any particular dive, depending on your level of training, recency of experience, and physical condition, as well as water conditions at the site. Remember that water conditions can change at any time, even during a dive. The rating system we've used is shown schematically in a chart in Chapter 3.

Thunderball Reef was the site used to film parts of the James Bond movie Thunderball.

This Spanish hogfish warily eyes the pursuing diver and oncoming photographer, typical of the area's bright tropical fish life.

1

Overview of New Providence Island

Though it has acquired the reputation of being tame and almost humdrum among the myriad Caribbean destinations, New Providence Island is what the Caribbean was, and is, all about.

Since the time of Columbus's first landfall on San Salvador in the Bahamas, this chain has played a central role in the history of the Western Hemisphere.

Called *baja mar*, or "shallow sea," by the Spanish, the islands were the gateway to the New World for more than 300 years.

The *baja mar* is one of the world's great maritime highways. Spanish galleons loaded with the wealth of the Indies, pirates and privateers, boatloads of colonists, great military armadas, wolfpacks of U-boats, and sleek cruise ships have all passed this way.

The earliest memories of an emerging New World live on in these islands. From the wharves of New Providence Island, supplies and trade goods moved to the colonies. Here cotton was traded for gunpowder by the blockade runners of the Civil War era, and rum runners loaded their wares during Prohibition. They live also in the historical sites of New Providence, such as Rawson Square where a statue of Queen Victoria overlooks the markets and streets of old Nassau. And they live in the local architecture, from the Government House to the high-tech hotels and office buildings that mark Nassau's emergence as an international center of offshore banking.

Though the thriving financial industry steadily increases, making tourists happy is the central and dominant business of the Bahamas. And New Providence is not only the political capital, it is also the chief tourist center as well. About 3.3 million entered the Bahamas in 1989, and well over a million of them went to Nassau.

Many of these tourists found Nassau and New Providence a satisfying compromise between the seclusion of an island vacation and the excitement of visiting a metropolitan center. But the sheer volume of visitors has tended to make serious divers discount the island's diving potential. In some folks' minds, a place that attracts a million people a year can't have virgin diving. They're wrong.

Windsurfing is another of Nassau's aquatic pleasures. The broad, shallow bays of the island's north side are the best places to run with the gentle trade winds.

Ironically, the dive resort building boom that went off in the Caribbean in the early 1970s bypassed New Providence altogether. But not because the diving isn't good. Many of those resorts were partially financed with aid from government development funds. Because of its booming tourist business, New Providence isn't the kind of place a government would spend public funds to develop diving. Most governments regard diving as a marginal tourist industry. Also, because diving is a marginal business when compared to general tourism, businesses on New Providence didn't make a special effort to attract divers. The islands that put the most emphasis on developing diving were largely those that had a small base of tourists to begin with, and fewer activities to attract tourists.

The result has been that, while some of the places that were virgin dive areas in the early 1970s have had their reefs stomped on and jet-finned into coral dust, the bare trickle of divers going into New Providence has left much of the island's submarine scenery pristine. This is particularly true of dive sites on the west and south sides of the island.

By plane or by boat, nearly a million visitors flood Nassau each year. The cruise ships dock at Prince George's Wharf in Nassau Harbour. The downtown area and historic district are just behind the Wharf.

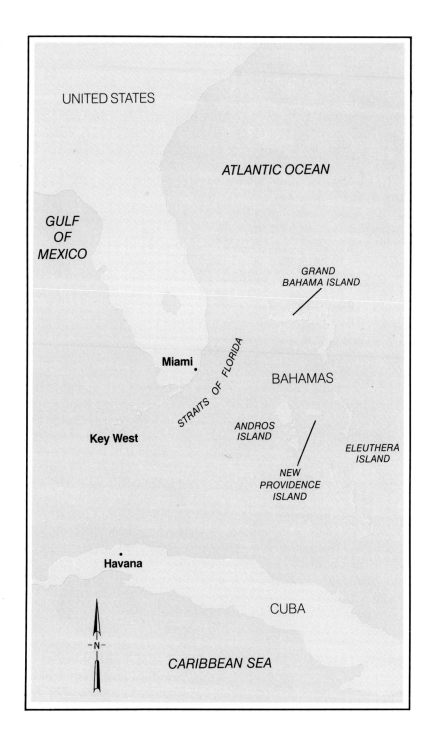

UNITED STATES

ATLANTIC OCEAN

GULF OF MEXICO

GRAND BAHAMA ISLAND

Miami

STRAITS OF FLORIDA

BAHAMAS

ANDROS ISLAND

Key West

ELEUTHERA ISLAND

NEW PROVIDENCE ISLAND

Havana

CUBA

–N–

CARIBBEAN SEA

Centered in the Eastern Caribbean, the Bahamas are the dry tops of a vast, shallow undersea plain called the Bahamas Bank.

Documents. If you're an American citizen, you won't need a passport to enter the Bahamas. You'll need proof of U.S. citizenship, such as a birth certificate or a voter's registration card. A driver's license is not acceptable as proof of citizenship.

The obvious cautions about carrying illicit drugs and handguns apply to the Bahamas. The customs folks are very serious about drugs and guns. If you carry any medication with you, be sure it's in a pharmacy container with the prescription still attached. It's rumored to be next to impossible to get a permit to bring in a handgun.

If you're flying home, you'll clear U.S. Customs at the airport in New Providence before boarding the plane. Things can get a little crowded on Fridays and Sundays, so leave some extra time and be prepared to wait in line. Once you go through U.S. Customs, you'll be directed to a departure lounge, and you can't leave the lounge without clearing Customs all over again.

Cruise Ships. A number of cruise ships call at Nassau. Carnival Cruise Lines owns the Crystal Palace Hotel complex at Cable Beach. If you're in the mood for a cruise, you can combine it with a stay on the island and get in some diving while you're there. Check with a travel agent for packages and fares, or call Carnival. The ships depart from Port Canaveral, Ft. Lauderdale, and Miami, FL.

Airlines. New Providence is served by a number of airlines and air charter companies. Competition is stiff and special fares abound. Packaged tours combining airfare with hotel accommodations are popular with visitors to Nassau, so a travel agent may be able to get you a better deal than you can get on your own. If you know who you'll be diving with, check with them first. If you're going as part of a group, they may be able to put you into a charter or into a block of seats on a commercial carrier.

Ask your travel agent to check with Bahamasair, the national carrier, too. Its fares are sometimes lower than the major U.S. carriers and the flights aren't normally crowded with tourists headed for the casinos on Paradise Island. Bahamasair flies to New Providence from Newark, NJ, Washington, DC and Philadelphia, as well as from Miami, Tampa, and Orlando, FL. If you plan to combine your trip to Nassau with a few days at one of the other dive destinations in the area, Bahamasair flies from Nassau to Freeport, Great Exuma, Eleuthera, Andros, Stella Maris, Crooked Island, San Salvador, Inagua, Mayaguana, and South Caicos.

At the time of publication, other scheduled air carriers with service to Nassau from the U.S. included Air Canada, Comair, Delta Airlines, Eastern Airlines, Eastern/Continental Express, Henson, Midway, Pan American, Piedmont/US Air, and TransWorld Airlines. Carnival Cruise Lines operates its own charter service, as does Paradise Island Airlines. Additional charter carriers include American Eagle, American Transair, and Club Med.

If you're in the mood for an aerial experience of a different nature, Chalk's International Airlines offers seaplane flights from Miami and Ft. Lauderdale to New Providence. The planes take off and land in Nassau Harbour, and Chalk's terminal is on Paradise Island.

Hotels. Nassau has been the winter retreat of rich Americans since at least the turn of the century. The result is a wide range of choices in types, styles, and prices of accommodations. There are ultra-luxurious high-rise hotels on Paradise Island, several of which were purchased by entertainer Merv Griffin in 1989. There are chains, including Sheraton, Holiday Inn, and Wyndham. And there dozens of small to medium-sized hotels, condominiums, and guest apartments from which to choose.

The dive operators on the island are unusually accommodating; no matter where you choose to stay, they'll send a bus around for you every morning, and return you to the hotel after your dives.

At the time of publication, three operators offered dive/hotel packages: Nassau Undersea Adventures, Dive Dive Dive, and Peter Hughes Dive South Ocean. If you intend to dive most of the days you're in Nassau, it will be worth your time to investigate them. Also, by combining accommodations with diving, you may get a better rate than if you purchase the two separately.

Nassau Undersea Adventures has a long-standing arrangement with the Orange Hill Inn, located across the street from a lovely—and often deserted—white sand beach on the north side of the island about fifteen minutes from downtown Nassau. The Inn is run by a charming British couple, Judy and Danny Lowe, who like and cater to divers. The units are clean and modern. (Many were brand-new as this edition went to press.) There's a large pool, satellite TV dish, and lush landscaping. Meals are served in a central dining room, and the lounge in the main building (which is sort of a living room/family room for the entire inn) is where the guests gather after dark.

The Divi Bahamas Beach Resort & Country Club, formerly known as South Ocean Beach, was acquired by the Divi hotel chain in 1987.

Peter Hughes Dive South Ocean operates the diving at Divi. The hotel has been thoroughly reconditioned and was in the process of completing 195 new luxury rooms at the time of publication. The resort is lavish, as are most of the Divi properties in the Caribbean, and offers an 18-hole golf course, lighted tennis courts, a marina, and a full watersports program (catamarans, jet skis, etc.) along with a full diving program.

Dive Dive Dive operates out of the Coral Harbour Hotel at Coral Harbour on the east end of New Providence. The hotel is a former apartment complex, with the rooms situated in separate bungalows. Each sleeps four and has a full kitchen with microwave oven.

If you're in the mood to sample a bit of nightlife, a bit of diving, and a lot of relaxing, you might consider the Paradise Island hotels or those at Cable Beach, such as the Crystal Palace. If you want old-money ambience and total luxury, Le Meridien has recently been refurbished. Be prepared to pay top dollar for these hotels, however, especially if you plan to visit in the winter. The paradox is that Nassau is very close to the U.S. mainland, so airfare is relatively inexpensive. However, the demand for land on New Providence is such that apartment rentals rival rates for similar units in Manhattan. As you can imagine, this makes land (and the hotels built on it) rather pricey.

The food in the big resort hotels is good, but of the prepackaged variety. And it's expensive, about $20 per person for dinner. Fortunately, there are a number of other restaurants on the island. At the less expensive level, there is a McDonald's in the shopping arcade of the British Colonial hotel, a Lum's on Bay Street, and a Taco Bell facing the cruise ship docks. Captain Nemo's, a seafood restaurant on east Bay Street, serves good food at reasonable prices. There are two Tony Roma's (steaks, ribs, seafood, hamburgers): one on Bay Street

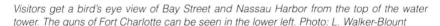

Visitors get a bird's eye view of Bay Street and Nassau Harbor from the top of the water tower. The guns of Fort Charlotte can be seen in the lower left. Photo: L. Walker-Blount

just across from the bridge to Paradise Island and one on West Bay Street outside of town. There are several pizza places, an English pub or two, and dozens of Bahamian restaurants, such as Choosy Foods off of Bay Street in Nassau and the Delaporte Bar on the north coast highway near Delaporte Point. A dinner of local seafood for four at the Delaporte can be had for about $20 total.

Nassau has something most diving destinations lack: true gourmet restaurants. The Graycliff, on West Hill Street near Government house is one. The food is superb, but if you think the hotel restaurants are expensive, wait until you see the Graycliff's menu. Bring your gold charge card. Prices run about $65 per person for dinner.

Shopping. Other than seafood and things made of conch shells, almost nothing originates in the Bahamas, so there are few true shopping bargains. Bay Street in Nassau is the shopping district, lined with small but elegant stores offering perfumes from Europe and America, electronics from Japan, and diamonds and emeralds from South America. Most of these items can be bought in the U.S. at comparable prices. There are some bargains on porcelain items made abroad, such as Lladro and Hummel figurines.

If you're an American who smokes cigars, you're in for a treat. You can actually sample something that the U.S. government won't let you have at home: a genuine Havana cigar. Certainly there are excellent cigars being made in the Dominican Republic, the Canary Islands, and Honduras, but none of them tastes *quite* like a Montecristo. At $7 per cigar, you'll likely be conservative in your purchases, but buy only what you can smoke during your vacation: It's very much against the rules to bring Cuban-made cigars into the U.S.

The straw market on Bay Street offers a unique shopping experience. If it can be made out of raffia or straw, you'll find it in this open-air arcade. Hundreds of craftspeople jam the area, offering rugs, hats, purses, and dolls, as well as shell jewelry and wood carvings. Remember to haggle; the first price offered is probably double the real selling price.

Currency. The Bahamas has its own currency system arranged on the U.S. model with a dollar divided into 100 pennies. The money looks terrific—very colorful and covered with exquisite calligraphic writing. You won't really need any, however, as U.S. dollars are accepted at par. You'll likely get change in Bahamian currency as you shop, but don't worry, it can be exchanged back into dollars before you leave. Keep enough for your departure tax at the airport ($15 per person at this writing) and a few bills for your collection at home.

History and Sightseeing

The Bahamas were initially discovered by a race of Indians, the Lucayans. Most likely, they were a branch of the Arawaks, a race of South American people that migrated up the Indies from the Orinoco River basin. During this journey up the archipelago, the Arawaks were just one step ahead of another group, the Caribs.

The Caribs, for whom the Caribbean Sea was named, were cannibals. From their homes in the lower Indies, they raided Arawak villages on Hispaniola, Cuba, the Virgin Islands, and in the Bahamas. Although they carried off men and women as slaves, reportedly killing those they couldn't carry with them, their efforts were paltry compared to those of the Europeans. The Lucayans of the Bahamas were used to work gold mines on Hispaniola, and less than a generation after the discovery of the Bahamas by Columbus, there were no more Lucayans.

The Europeans. By 1646, the English, well established on Bermuda to the north, considered the Bahamas as Crown property. Land grants were made to encourage colonizations. But the islands, all rock and sand with little fertile soil, were hard on men and animals.

Paradise Island is a primary focus of activity. The Resorts International casino, hotel, and convention center complex also includes gourmet restaurants, a discotheque, and show theatre. Marinas, shopping, and a seaplane terminal make Paradise Island almost a self-contained resort.

The first major industry to succeed was *wrecking*, the practice of salvaging wrecked merchant ships.

These salvors were not above occasionally extinguishing the light in a lighthouse, or building a fire far inland to lure ships onto the shallow reefs of the Bahama Bank.

In addition to the wreckers, Nassau was for several decades the lair of some of the hemisphere's most desperate pirates. During the periodic wars that flared between England, France, and Spain in the 17th and 18th centuries, the English often granted sea captains the right to pillage enemy shipping without being subject to a charge of piracy. These private naval vessels, or privateers, were not quick to give up sacking Spanish or French ships when a truce was declared.

Nassau became the home port of many of these rascals. In fact, during the War of the Spanish Succession and for four years afterward, from 1703 until 1714, Nassau was governed by the pirates. Edward Teach, remembered as Blackbeard, was one of the most prominent.

After numerous complaints from the Spanish, England sent a naval hero, Captain Woodes Rogers, to evict the pirates. His accomplishment is commemorated by the street in front of Prince George's Wharf, now called Woodes Rogers Walk.

Smuggling has a prominent place in the modern history of the Bahamas as well. During Prohibition in the U.S., liquor from Europe was shipped to Nassau, where it was transferred to freighters, airplanes, and fast coastal boats. The ragtag flotilla deceived, outran, or outfought the Coast Guard, bringing load after load of alcoholic libations to the speakeasies of a thirsty America.

The government of the Bahamas profited as handsomely as the rumrunners. It doubled its tax on liquor imports. Every case that came through Nassau deposited a hefty sum in the colony's coffers. Massive public works projects, including Prince George's Wharf, where the cruise ships now dock, and the municipal water tower, were built with liquor tax revenues.

Some farsighted businessmen saw in this new wealth a way for the islands to become self sufficient. Wealthy Americans had begun spending the winter season in Nassau at the turn of the century. Now, with the liquor revenues, the capital was available to build facilities to better serve these tourists and to advertise to attract more. The Bahamas was thus set on the path it still follows. The heavy liquor tax was eventually repealed, but rising revenues from tourism encouraged Great Britain to consider the colony self sufficient, and in 1973, the Bahamas became independent under the leadership of Prime Minister Lynden O. Pindling.

An enjoyable day can be spent in visiting the cluster of historic sites and buildings which trace the history of Nassau. An excellent guide to the historic district, Pictorial Nassau, is available at newsstands and bookstores all over the island.

2

Diving In New Providence Island

When divers talk about the shrines of scuba, Nassau is not normally mentioned. If you want to know what you're missing, there's a quick way to find out: If you've ever seen any of the numerous James Bond movies with underwater scenes (*Thunderball*, *Dr. No*, and *Never Say Never Again*) or if you remember the TV series *Flipper*, then you've already seen what diving around New Providence is like.

New Providence has been a popular location for motion pictures for at least four decades. Underwater scenes for the 1950s version of *20,000 Leagues Under The Sea* were shot inshore from the Clifton Wall. Parts of *Splash!* were filmed here, as was *Wet Gold*. Ron Howard (who directed *Splash!*) must have liked the place because he returned to shoot the water scenes for *Cocoon* in 1985. There may be more film of these reefs than of any others in the world, but there seem to be plenty of fresh backgrounds to keep the directors coming back. The legendary Jordan Klein—who filmed many of the underwater scenes in the Bond pictures—was shooting a commercial during our stay on the island in January 1990.

The reasons they choose Nassau are good reasons for you to consider it as well.

New Providence is close to the U.S. and is easily reached via scheduled airlines. Also, because there are direct flights from major U.S. cities, the airfare is comparatively low. The weather is dependable—very good during most of the year—and there's always a lee when the wind does kick up for a day or two. And one more reason: There's excellent diving here. There are shallow reefs and walls, sponges and corals, shipwrecks and sunken airplanes. Add the bountiful population of fish and frequent appearance of large pelagic animals like stingrays and you have classic Caribbean diving.

The diving is well organized by professional operators with solid rental gear, fast boats, and stable, knowledgeable divemasters. If you choose New Providence, be prepared to shock your peers when you get home with stories of deep walls, huge sponges, mammoth groupers, and famous movie sets. They may not believe you saw all that in New Providence. But remember, you have proof—just tell them to go rent *Thunderball* at the video store and check it out.

Sponges, mounding corals, and deepwater gorgonians decorate the vertical edges of the Clifton Wall, along the south shore of New Providence. ◊

North Side Diving

Nassau is located on the north side of New Providence, and most of the major hotels are here or on Paradise Island, slightly east and north of Nassau proper. Nassau and the Paradise Island hotels are the center of action, with restaurants, nightclubs, and shops clustered around the harbor area.

The diving most convenient to these hotels is also on the north side. Most of the sites here are either shallow coral gardens or wrecks. The two operators located on the north side, Sun Divers and Bahama Divers, don't often dive on the south side—it's a 45-minute run from the harbor and, with any wind at all, a rough ride. Primarily, they stick to the north side sites. When the wind blows, they dive the shallows in the lee of Athol Island and Rose Island.

Bahamas Divers is located on east Bay Street, very near the foot of the Paradise Island Bridge. The shop has a fairly complete selection of gear for sale or rent. Instruction can be arranged, either a full course or quick familiarization, and they offer the same basic services as Sun Divers. Bahamas Divers docks their two boats at the marina at the north end of the Paradise Island Bridge, just to the left of the toll booths on Paradise Island.

As with Sun Divers, most of the trips are to sites on the north side—the shallows near Athol Island or the various wrecks and reefs fronting Paradise Island.

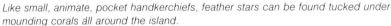

Like small, animate, pocket handkerchiefs, feather stars can be found tucked under mounding corals all around the island.

The LCT wreck on the north side of New Providence offers a spectacular first wreck dive to novices and beautiful coral growth for more experienced divers.

Sun Divers operates from a shop on the beach at the British Colonial on Bay Street in downtown Nassau. Their boats leave the dock daily at 9 a.m. for a single-tank dive, and at 1 p.m. for a two-tank dive. On the way out to the site, they pick up divers from docks around the harbor and at Paradise Island.

The operation is owned by Steve Sweeting and Lambert Albury. You can usually find them at the shop before the morning dive or just before the afternoon dive leaves. They have three boats, two custom 55-footers and a 30-footer. The boats are big and beamy, so they ride well and are set up for comfortable diving.

For novices or non-divers, Sun Divers offers a pool check-out followed by a dive, all gear included, for one price. The dives are the same price whether you bring your own gear or use theirs.

Sun Divers also caters to snorkelers, especially on trips to the shallows around Athol Island.

The run from the British Colonial dock to the close-in sites such as the LCT wreck is very short, so it's easy to squeeze in a quick dive even if you're only staying the weekend. The north side of the island lacks the spectacular drop-offs seen along the Clifton Wall, but if diving isn't the main item on your itinerary, the wrecks and reefs here are well worth seeing.

Dive Dive Dive is located in the Coral Harbour Hotel at Coral Harbour on the west end of New Providence. There are accommodations for 20 at the hotel, which is on a short canal that feeds into the ocean. Dive Dive Dive picks up divers from any hotel on New Providence for day trips to the south side sites including the Bond wrecks, the Pumpkin Patch, and even out to the buoy in the Tongue of the Ocean.

Nassau Undersea Adventures is owned and operated by Stuart Cove, an affable Canadian who grew up on New Providence. Cove has helped with the location work of many of the feature films shot in Nassau—*Never Say Never Again, Cocoon, Wet Gold, Splash!*—and has been involved in sinking several of the wrecks that attract divers to the south side of the island.

The shop is located inside the ultra-exclusive Lyford Cay development. Burly security guards man the iron gates, behind which lie the Caribbean retreats of celebrities such as Sean Connery and Diana Ross. If you want a peek at the *real* lifestyles of the rich and famous, take a dive with Nassau Undersea Adventures.

The operation runs four boats including a beamy 45-footer and a flat-top. There are two fast boats for reaching the sites farther offshore. The Clifton Wall and Goulding Cay are less than 15 minutes from the dock, so there's no long ride to deal with, and as the south side of the island is normally the lee, the water is usually flat. There's plenty of well-maintained rental gear available if you prefer to travel light, along with some underwater photo equipment. Divemaster J.P. "Doc" Genasi videotapes many of the dives, so you can buy a tape of yourself in action ducking under a huge ray or petting a silky shark out at the buoy in Tongue of the Ocean to show the folks back home. Multiple groups are accommodated easily, and Nassau Undersea Adventures offers air/land/dive packages from major U.S. gateways.

The ambiance is low-key, friendly, and relaxed, but thoroughly professional. The crew is made up largely of locals—divers born and raised on New Providence—and their knowledge of the area is superb. They're also very accommodating; if you have a special request (big groupers, big sponges, rays), they probably know just the right spot to indulge your fancy. They can even fix you up a date with a herd of sharks out at the buoy in Tongue of the Ocean.

Peter Hughes Dive South Ocean is located on the grounds of the Divi Bahamas Beach Resort & Country Club, formerly known as South Ocean Beach. As with all the Peter Hughes operations, this one is well-equipped, courteous, and efficient.

The dive center is at the resort's marina and is very new. The

A huge Southern stingray buzzes a diver at The Runway, one of the many popular sites along the Clifton Wall on the south side of New Providence.

buildings include a classroom, rental area, and retail store, plus a full E-6 photo lab for processing Ektachrome slides. You can rent anything you don't feel like bringing—from mask and snorkel to Nikonos cameras and video gear. There's even a video editing facility, and instruction in still photography and video is available.

The Clifton Wall is directly offshore from the resort, but the quarter- to half-mile distance to the sites and the occasional commercial vessel heading to or from the Clifton Pier dictate boat diving rather than dives from shore.

Dive South Ocean also runs four boats, all of which are big, seaworthy and very comfortable, even in the occasional chop. The close-in sites are no more than 15 minutes from the dock and the operation also runs to Goulding Cay (around the west end of the island) and to sites further offshore, including the buoy in the Tongue of the Ocean.

The resort itself is delightful, with restaurants, bars, an 18-hole golf course, and lighted tennis courts. For the non-diver there are jet skis, catamarans, and windsurfing. It's an "all-inclusive" style resort, and though you won't have to leave the grounds during your stay, Nassau is only about 25 minutes away by public bus.

Any way you cut it, you can't go wrong with the operators on Nassau. You can pick and choose, diving with each one for a few days, or take a package with one operator for your entire stay.

Conservation and the Bahamas Marine Park

It is the obligation of every diver to minimize their impact on the undersea environment. Although every dive inevitably results in some disruption or even damage to the dive area, being aware of a few simple principles will make you a better diver and less of a risk to the playground beneath the sea.

Buoyancy. The most obvious, but least understood, principle is to remain neutrally buoyant. Neutral buoyancy means just that. A diver wearing the right amount of weight, with just a puff of air in their buoyancy compensator, will neither rise nor sink. While neutrally buoyant, the diver can hover over, rather than crawl through, growth on the seafloor. Although coral looks very solid, it is in fact the fragile tissue of living animals. Dangling depth gauges and octopus regulators can bang into hard corals, killing polyps or producing scars which may become infected with coral-killing sponge or algae. Hoses and straps can also get tangled in soft corals, uprooting them or tearing their plumes. Nothing is so destructive as a herd of overly heavy divers scrambling and scraping over a reef. Don't hesitate to ask the advice of a dive guide about how much weight to wear.

Flippers. Watch those fin tips. The big power fins favored by most divers act like a McCormack reaper when churned by a pair of human legs. It's incredibly easy to break off the tips of branching corals or edges of sheet corals by thrashing them with jet fins. While diving, be aware that your feet actually end about 12 inches beyond your toes, at the edge of your fins. Also be careful not to get so close to the sand that you kick it up off the bottom. Besides ruining the visibility for everyone else on the dive, the sand can settle on corals, making their tenuous lives that much more difficult. If you want to get down in the sand to observe something, look around to ensure you have a clear area to settle down. Go in vertically, like a landing helicopter, and touch the sand gently or hover just above its surface. When you're ready to move on, don't just kick off. Instead, inhale to give yourself extra buoyancy and use your hand to push away from the bottom before kicking with your fins.

Fishery Laws of the Bahamas

The government of the Bahamas has taken a number of steps to preserve and protect the islands' ocean resources. The laws listed here are those that most concern divers, but are by no means a comprehensive list. If you plan to fish extensively while in New Providence, you may want to write the Ministry of Tourism for a complete copy of fishing regulations. Particularly if you plan on spearfishing, you will want to know the laws. No spearfishing of any sort is allowed while using scuba, and powered spearguns are not allowed into the country. If you put a powered speargun in your luggage, it's very likely the Bahamian customs officials will impound it.

- No poisons may be used to catch or kill fish.

- No marine animals or products may be taken with the use of underwater breathing equipment.

- Hawaiian slings or pole spears are the only type of spearing devices snorkel divers may use. Powered spearguns may not be used.

- The export of any marine animal or product is illegal unless a permit has been obtained.

- No marine animals or products may be removed from the north coast of New Providence from Goulding Cay in the west to a line drawn between the eastern tip of Athol Island and the eastern end of New Providence, and inside of a line drawn through the fringing islands. In the Exuma Cays Land and Sea Park no commercial fishing is allowed.

3

New Providence Dive Sites

The sites around New Providence fall into three basic categories: shallow reefs, deeper reefs and walls, and wrecks. Due to the generally benign water conditions around the island, most of the sites are accessible to divers at any level of experience.

The chart (page 32) does recommend some dives, mostly the deeper and wall dives only for more experienced divers. With proper supervision, many of these are suitable for novices as well.

There is very little opportunity for unsupervised shore diving around New Providence. Most of the sites are too far from shore to swim to. Although this may not suit the most ardent four-dive-per-day diver, the boat rides are short and pleasant. The boats in use by the operators are generally fast, comfortable, and well set up for diving. The boat diving also contributes to the admirable safety record of the island's dive operators, as there is a guide along on virtually every dive done by visitors.

If you haven't been diving in the past year, or if you think your skills might be a little rusty, talk to the dive operators. They don't expect everyone who comes to New Providence to be an expert diver. They're used to helping refresh people's memories. You'll be more comfortable and have a better vacation if you let the operators do what you're paying them to do—help.

Although it shines brilliantly when lit by a photographer's strobe, even the brightest sponge looks grayish when viewed without artificial light. The sponges of New Providence are so varied and colorful, it's worth carrying a flashlight to reveal their true colors. ⬦

DIVE SITE RATINGS

	Novice Diver	Novice w/Instructor or divemaster	Intermediate Diver	Intermediate w/Instructor or divemaster	Advanced Diver	Advanced w/Instructor or divemaster
South Side						
1 Clifton Wall			X	X	X	
2 Will Laurie Wreck			X	X	X	
3 Will Laurie Wall			X	X	X	
4 Sand Chute			X	X	X	
5 The Bond Wrecks	X	X	X	X	X	
6 20,000 Leagues*	X	X	X	X	X	
7 Porpoise Pens		X	X	X	X	
8 Cessna Wreck		X	X	X	X	
9 Pumpkin Patch		X	X	X	X	
10 The Runway	X	X	X	X	X	
11 The Buoy			X	X	X	
North Side						
12 LCT Wreck*	X	X	X	X	X	
13 Trinity Caves		X	X	X	X	
14 Mahoney Wreck	X	X	X	X	X	
15 Thunderball Reef	X	X	X	X	X	
16 Alcora Wreck	X	X	X	X	X	
17 Balmoral Island*	X	X	X	X	X	

*Denotes good snorkeling spots

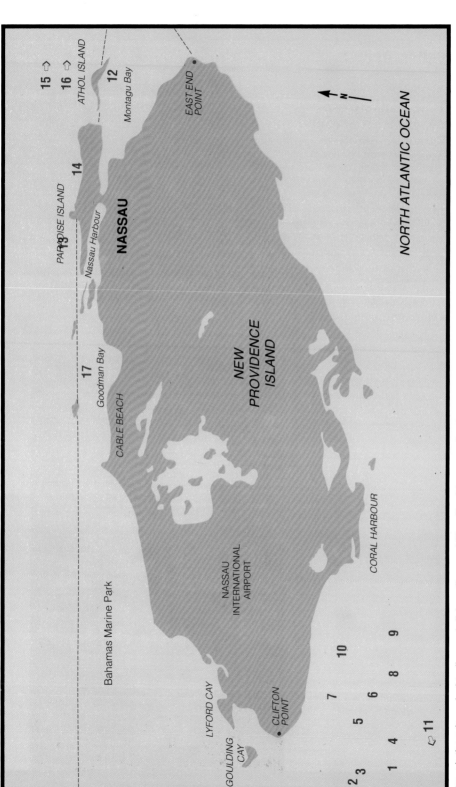

Though there is undoubtedly good diving all around New Providence, so far the two clusters of dive sites noted on the map have provided more than enough scenery to keep visitors busy.

Clifton Wall   1

Typical depth range	:	50-90 ft. (15-28 m)
Typical current conditions	:	slight
Expertise required	:	intermediate
Access	:	boat

The Clifton Wall is host to a number of New Providence's best dive sites. Clifton is a true wall; the general topography is a wide, sandy shelf extending ½-1 mile offshore (1-1½ km) gradually sloping down to 40 or 50 feet. Scattered coral heads litter the shelf for 20-30 yards (18-28 meters) shoreward of the lip.

The lip of the wall varies in depth. At some places it's as shallow as 45 feet (13 meters). At others, it dips to 80 or 90 feet (28 meters) before going entirely vertical.

The Clifton Wall is a vertical escarpment of mounding coral that runs nearly a third the length of New Providence about a half mile off the south shore.

Knots of sponge colonies are common along the Clifton Wall. This tangle includes at least three species: a large basket, purple tubes, and red, purple, and yellow rope sponges.

Most of the coral is of the encrusting forms—star, mountainous star, and sheet corals—and the growth is impressive. The lip is riddled with crevices, undercuts, ledges, and chutes. Large tube sponges, especially yellow tubes, dangle into these declivities. Vase and basket sponges are also spotted around the lip and edge of the dropoff. The wall has a truly impressive number of rope sponges, again the yellow-green ones predominating over red and purple. There are very few large sea fans, but other forms of soft coral—sea whips, sea plumes, deepwater gorgonians—are plentiful.

Although the area is fished fairly heavily, large tropicals abound. At an unnamed site opposite the Porpoise Pens, two of the largest gray angels that ever graced a Caribbean reef are regular performers.

The wall attracts a lot of groupers, from big ones up to 4 or 5 feet (1.5 meters) to smaller ones of about a foot (0.3 meter) in length. All varieties can be seen, too; from monster blackfin and marble groupers down to shoebox-sized coneys, Nassaus, and tigers.

Other large pelagics are often seen here, as well. The occasional shark is joined by larger numbers of big rays. Smaller Southern stingrays park in the gullies between the shallow patch reefs, so watch those flippers on the shallow dives.

A striking feature of this area is the sheer size and variety of the animals. They aren't hand-fed, so they're a little skittish, but by patiently stalking you should be able to get close enough for a decent photo.

Animals that filter their food from the water thrive in the rich current that sweeps along the edge of the Clifton Wall.

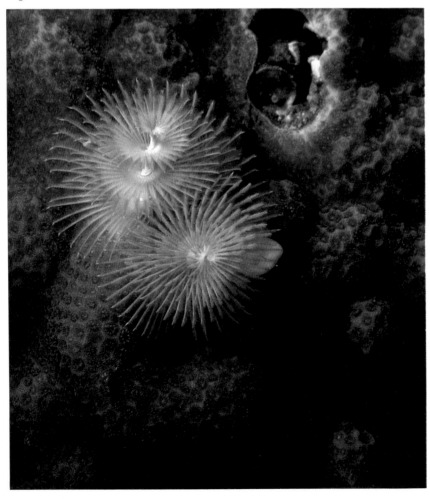

A distant relative of the graceful starfish, the sea cucumber may be the most unsightly member of the vast echinoderm family. Photo: H. Taylor.

The whole catalog of Caribbean tropicals is represented here, either near the wall or in the shallows just shoreward. In a few outings you'll see tang, bar jacks, Spanish hogfish, hog snappers, yellowtails, graysbys, rock beauties, French-striped grunts, squirrelfish, damsels, trumpetfish, diamond blennies, royal grammas, porkfish, spadefish, spotted butterflyfish, French angels, gobies, sea cucumbers; basically whatever you're looking for.

A lot of cleaning activity goes on here, as well. Tiger groupers at cleaning stations are very approachable, and while you might not be able to fill the frame of your 1:1 macro framer with a goby working over the lower lip of a coney, try using a 28mm or 35mm lens on your Nikonos for some head-and-fins shots.

Generally, the visibility on the wall is good, ranging from 50 feet (15 meters) in windy weather right on up to 150 feet (50 meters) or more.

Typical depth range	:	70 ft. (22 m)
Typical current conditions	:	none
Expertise required	:	novice with divemaster
Access	:	boat

If you're getting the impression that you could walk across the bottom just by stepping from wreck to wreck, you wouldn't be far from wrong. Nassau is literally ringed by wrecks—both accidental and intentional.

The *Will Laurie*, a 150-foot (46 meter) freighter, is of recent vintage, having been sunk in 1988. A memorial not only to early 20th century ocean trade but apparently to community property laws as well, the ship was christened in London in 1909 as the *Will Mary*. Sometime later, it became the *Will Laurie*. In 1988 it came to rest rather abruptly on the Clifton Pier on the south side of New Providence. A salvage company offered to remove the vessel from the wharf for a large sum of money, but before the government accepted, the ship disappeared.

The pilothouse of the Will Laurie *looks a bit ransacked but still operable, despite being under 70 feet (22 m) of seawater.*

The cargo holds of the Will Laurie *are wide open, and they provide ample surprises for divers who've a mind to rummage.*

An unconfirmed rumor has it that the Underseas Adventures crew, inspired by an excess of holiday cheer, drug the *Will Laurie* off the dock in the middle of the night and sank it just about due south of Clifton Point.

The *Will Laurie* has wide-open cargo holds and a small wheelhouse perched on the stern. Steel railings support what's left of an awning on the short afterdeck and one can almost imagine the crew huddled in its shade, sipping lukewarm beer and trying to survive the stifling heat and tedium of what must have been a very long crossing from England to New Providence.

Typical depth range	:	60-80 ft. (18-24 m)
Typical current conditions	:	none
Expertise required	:	intermediate
Access	:	boat

The *Will Laurie* Wall is an especially nice section of the Clifton Wall near the *Will Laurie*. The reef is very, very vertical and the water is usually quite clear. Keep an eye on those depth gauges: It's easy to keep on sinking, watching the thick tapestry of corals unroll, until you're too deep to do anything about it.

The usual plan is to dive the face of the wall, swimming away from the boat at about 80 feet (24 meters), then come back along the top of the wall, which is as shallow as 40 feet (12 meters) in places.

Once you've gotten your thrills hanging off the wall, save some bottom time and air for the top; it's a nice reef. Though the growth is low, there are dozens of parrot fish here, along with big Nassau groupers and yellowtails too numerous to count. The guides have been feeding the fish here for several years, so your body hitting the

It seems redundant to say that there are a lot of Nassau groupers in Nassau, but their sheer abundance makes it unavoidable. Some are quite brazen and will even pose.

The Will Laurie *Wall is extemely vertical and its lip is crowded by hordes of hungry yellow-tails, groupers, and surgeon fish.*

water sounds a lot like dinner to the throngs of marine life below. Proffering the barest morsel attracts clouds of yellowtails, who seem to be able to fight off the surgeon fish, hog snappers, and smaller tropicals, keeping the choice bits among themselves.

The Sand Chute 4

Typical depth range	:	50-90 ft. (15-28 m)
Typical current conditions	:	slight
Expertise required	:	intermediate
Access	:	boat

Along the Clifton Wall is a site called the Chute—a large crevasse in the wall with sand spilling through. The lip of the wall is shallow here, about 40 feet (12 meters). The Chute is a vast trough, 20 feet (6 meters) deep and at least 20 feet wide. It breaches the mounding-coral lip and continues down into the abyss.

On the west side is an overhang and two tunnels which are just big enough for a smallish diver to crawl through. The tunnels join under the reef and exit through a chimney about 15 feet (5 meters) long onto the top of the reef.

Sand falls, such as the Chute, are formed by similar, though opposite forces to those which create gullies on land. Gullies are created by uncontrolled water runoff while sand falls are formed on steep underwater slopes by sand constantly moving over the edge of a cliff. This movement prevents reef building animals from taking hold and creating a barrier to hold back the sand.

A nest of purple, red, and yellow rope sponges near the Chute displays a variety matched by few Caribbean destinations except Jamaica.

Be careful going through the Chute area, as the sand bottom is very fine and loose. Use the cave diver's technique of jabbing two fingers into the sand and pulling yourself through, rather than using fins, so as not to silt out the Chute and tunnel for those behind you.

Use buoyancy to rise through the chimney, and watch your tank on the ceiling of the cave. Tank valves can do a number on the thin edges of plate corals that overlap into the tunnel.

If you're the first diver in the Chute, check out the chimney and entrance to the cave. The critters think it's a pretty neat place, too. You may find a luxury-sized grouper or perhaps some squirrelfish lounging about before the humans come.

Typical depth range	:	30-50 ft. (10-15 m)
Typical current conditions	:	none
Expertise required	:	novice
Access	:	boat

The story line of the James Bond film *Never Say Never Again* called for a wreck. The crew found a terrific 100-foot (34-meter) freighter known as the *Tears of Allah*. It has a beautiful rounded pilothouse up forward, a short bow, a long cabin with easy access, a broad fantail, and plenty of hatches. In short, it's a perfect wreck. Seized as a dope runner by the Bahamian government, the boat was sunk here by the film crew with the help of Nassau Underseas Adventures owner Stuart Cove.

A visiting diver peers into the large after cabin of the Tears of Allah. *The hull is pretty clean*

Unlike the older wrecks on the north side of New Providence, this steel wreck hasn't yet developed a full coating of marine growth, but the nearly-intact freighter is a stunning shallow-water wreck dive.

Sitting upright in 50 feet (15 meters) of water on a sand bottom, the boat is easily viewed from the surface. From the top it looks small, but once you're down, the size begins to impress. Being the first one down will ensure a silt-free photo of the wheelhouse, as most divers tend to crawl, rather than float, through the large, glassless windows. The algae now covering the wreck holds a lot of sand, and it doesn't take much to kick it up. If you're a serious photographer, take a model and try to get out on the wreck with as few other divers as possible. It's the single most photogenic wreck in this part of the Caribbean. That's more than one man's opinion; three television commercials and yet another full-length feature—*Wet Gold*—have been filmed here.

If silt becomes a problem, move to the west side and look back toward the boat. About amidships, the remains of a wooden dinghy protrude from the sand. With a wide-angle lens, you can take in the graceful curve of the dinghy's sides, the entire wreck, and dozens of garden eels waving in the sand between.

A few dozen yards away are the remains of the airplane prop created for *Thunderball*. The script called for a jet fighter armed with

These squirrelfish, like squirrelfish the world over, are shy creatures which prefer night to day. Their large eyes help them see in the dark.

Though it looks like an overgrown schoolyard jungle gym, this was actually one of the sets used in the James Bond thriller Thunderball.

nuclear missiles to be hijacked and hidden on the sea floor. The "fighter" was made from steel pipes and fiberglass. The skin is now gone, leaving what appears to be a huge erector set. Every square inch of the frame is carpeted with gorgonians, giving the effect of a fuzzy set of monkey bars.

Large basket stars cling to the gorgonians. To one side of the airplane is an enormous clump of brain coral. The fish here are fed pretty regularly and are more tame. A green anemone with tentacles as big around as your thumb lives in one of the side pockets of the coral head.

Typical depth range	:	15-25 ft. (5-8 m)
Typical current conditions	:	none
Expertise required	:	novice
Access	:	boat

One of the inshore dives off the Clifton Wall is called 20,000 Leagues Under the Sea, after the movie of the same name.

20,000 Leagues is a coral garden with a difference. The spur-and-groove reef here is very well developed, with the walls of the spurs reaching up 10 feet (3 meters) from the sand channels between. These channels are, in places, so narrow a diver has a hard time squeezing through. The channels twist and wind in an almost serpentine pattern.

The narrow gullies of the shallow 20,000 Leagues area abound with brilliant tropicals, such as this queen angel. Photo: H. Taylor.

Though shallow, 20,000 Leagues is subject to very little surge. The calm water and small life forms that infest the crevices make it an excellent spot for macrophotography.

By following the bottom, you get an impression of what it must be like to fly through the Grand Canyon in a helicopter.

The fish life here is the attraction. Small tropicals mob the many crevices, and larger game—particularly Nassau groupers—park for a rest in the undercuts at the base of the spurs. The area is visited sometimes by large leopard rays and jumbo blackfin groupers.

The whole patch must encompass several acres, and it runs almost all of the way out to the edge of the wall. If you're a photographer, try lying on your back or sitting down in one of the sand channels while divers swim over the tops of the spurs. Light the sides of the spur and the divers with a strobe and you'll get something that resembles a good wall shot, only with more light and brighter water.

Typical depth range	:	40-90 ft. (12-28 m)
Typical current conditions	:	none
Expertise required	:	novice
Access	:	boat

This spot is just opposite the pens where the underwater sequences for *Flipper* were filmed. The pens are still in the water, adjacent to the shore, and were used last year for the underwater sequences of *Cocoon*. Ric O'feldman—diver, amateur cetologist, and part–time filmmaker— trained and worked with Flipper, but for this movie, several porpoises were caught in Exuma and a trainer was brought in from the Florida Keys.

The Porpoise Pens area is just offshore from an underwater corral that was used to film sequences for the TV series Flipper and parts of the movie Cocoon. Photo: H. Taylor

A fabulous black coral bush clings to an outcropping on the wall at Porpoise Pens. Black coral jewelry is available in Nassau, and though it can legally be imported into the U.S., conscientious divers won't encourage the abuse of this resource by buying it.

The Porpoise Pens is a deep dive along the wall, with the lip beginning at about 40 feet (12 meters) and a lot of the scenery at 70 to 80 feet (22 to 25 meters).

At these depths, the true dimensions of the wall are apparent. Inky blue-blackness laps at your fins from below. On the wall, as if displayed in a submarine gallery, are splash after splash of aquatic art: a swirling deepwater gorgonian recalling Van Gogh, a pastiche of encrusting sponge fetching up images of Jackson Pollock.

Although black coral jewelry is sold in various shops on the island, it doesn't appear as though this part of the reef has been stripped of the semi-precious stuff. There are several bushes located in the 70 foot (22 meter) range here.

Be careful with your depth gauge. It's very easy to get excited by an oversized sponge, or be enticed into diving after a grouper and end up at 110 feet plus plus plus. The divemasters on New Providence are safety conscious and will give you full information about each dive before you enter the water. But if you have any question about your own skills, stick close to the dive leader. He'll probably be able to show you the better parts of the reef, as well.

Cessna Wreck 8

Typical depth range	:	40 ft. (12 m)
Typical current conditions	:	none
Expertise required	:	novice with divemaster
Access	:	boat

This wreck is just one more example of the handiwork of those prolific James Bond film crews. The script for *Never Say Never Again* required Sean Connery to crash-land a small twin-engine plane in the ocean, then escape. For the underwater sequences, this wreck was hauled out to within a hundred yards of the Clifton Wall and sunk. It is, as you might expect, the picture-perfect plane wreck. Most of the plexiglass windscreen was removed, so it's safe enough to climb in through the open passenger door and sit in the pilot's seat.

The plane sits in an open sand patch, so if you're with other divers get down quick if you want clear photos before the area gets silted out.

This twin-engine plane was sunk as a prop for Never Say Never Again *and it's still a perfect prop for photographers.*

A small tunnel, just big enough for a diver to squeeze through, starts at the top of the wall straight out from the plane wreck, exiting on the face of the wall at about 60 ft. (23 m).

A low reef grows between the plane and the wall. It's pretty typical of other areas along Clifton Wall with the exception of a tunnel, which starts at about 45 feet (13 meters) and comes out on the wall at about 60 feet (18 meters).

There are some large ear sponges along this section of the wall, and Nassau groupers are commonly seen skulking among the coral heads at the edge of the drop off.

Typical depth range	:	40-80 ft. (13-24 m)
Typical current conditions	:	none
Expertise required	:	intermediate
Access	:	boat

As the cluster of dive sites on the map might suggest, you can drop an anchor almost anywhere on the Clifton Wall and find excellent diving. The Pumpkin Patch is a small section that displays beautiful purple tube sponges. The ones in Bonaire may be a little bigger or a little more plentiful, but these are plenty big enough for visiting divers to get excited about. The area is crowded with parrot fish, too, and the profusion of stoplight and queen parrots makes a nice tropical addition to the marine landscape.

The Pumpkin Patch lies just at the edge of the wall, so it makes a good first or second dive. If you do it as a first dive, you can cruise down to 80 feet and look back up at the cascade of plate corals, tube, and ear sponges trickling down the face of the wall. If you've already

The Pumpkin Patch was named for the mounding corals found along the wall here.

To those who scoff that they just don't grow them big in New Providence, these purple tube sponges provide a vivid display of almost Bonairean proportions—longer than the outstretched limbs of this diver.

incurred some residual nitrogen time, the top of the wall is just as nice. In addition to parrots, grouper are plentiful, as are surgeon fish and the omnipresent yellowtails. We saw some interesting behavior here: a trumpetfish swimming arched over the back of a grouper. The grouper was trying to get cleaned, but every time á cleaner got anywhere near the grouper, the trumpetfish sucked it in.

Typical depth range	:	30 ft. (9 m)
Typical current conditions	:	none
Expertise required	:	novice
Access	:	boat

Some divers get their thrills from going deep, some from shallow coral gardens, some from well-preserved wrecks. But before you name your favorite, you have to try The Runway. It's not much to look at; just a small oval patch of scruffy coral heads surrounded by powdery white sand. It's what happens at The Runway that will thrill you.

It seems a mass of grammas, wrasse, gobies, and other parasite-eating species have set up shop here; a veritable strip-mall of cleaning services. Larger animals who feel the need come in and circle over the coral heads a few dozen times while the little guys munch the copepods and such off their skin.

For some reason, The Runway is especially popular with Southern stingrays. Big rays. Six- to eight-foot-wingspan stingrays.

A resident barracuda called Barry entertains divers waiting for the main show—big stingrays—at The Runway.

Although the dive operators obviously can't guarantee a timely performance by the rays, this one showed up about five minutes after we dropped anchor. Rays are normally pretty skittish around divers but while being cleaned, they totally ignored us.

The boat will drop you a few yards off the patch on the sand bottom. If there are no rays in attendance, you can play with Barry the barracuda (a healthy three-footer) or poke around under the coral heads looking for morays. The eels here are emphatically *not* tame and have nipped one or two of the unwary.

The main attraction at The Runway is the stingrays, which flap in from the direction of the wall and slowly circle the coral heads. The experience of having a six- to eight-foot (3-4 meter) ray swimming within a yard of your face mask is unforgettable. On our dive, a ray's wings actually brushed a diver's video camera housing on one pass. If you like rays, you'll absolutely love The Runway.

Typical depth range	:	30 ft. (9 m)
Typical current conditions	:	none
Expertise required	:	intermediate with divemaster
Access	:	boat

Okay. You say you've been to Cayman, you've been to the Red Sea, you've been to Truk Lagoon, you've been to Palau **and Yap. Sure** Nassau has lush coral and pretty fishes, but you're looking for something that can get your heart rate above 30. Would swimming in the Tongue of the Ocean with a gaggle of sharks do it for you?

This is definitely not an outing for the faint at heart. **The Tongue** of the Ocean is a trench just over two miles deep that **reaches up past** Andros, dead-ending south of New Providence, dividing the Bahama

Getting up close and personal with a shark is some folks' idea of a good time. If you're one of them, The Buoy should be your next port of call. Photo: S. Cove

Unlike shark dives where guides put your back up against a reef, ask you not to move, and then bait in one or two or the toothsome predators, this is a virtual free-for-all with the closest point of solid land being two miles straight down. Photo: S. Cove

Bank in half. Several years ago, the U.S. Navy moved one of its sonar buoys from Deer Island to a new location in Tongue of the Ocean. The buoy attracted some little fish and they told two friends, and they told two friends, and so on and so on. Before long all these little fish under the buoy had attracted some really big fish—a gang of silky sharks with an occasional hammerhead or mako mixed in for good measure.

Stuart Cove of Nassau Undersea Adventures began diving on the buoy several years ago. The experience was so exciting that he decided to share it with visiting divers.

The trip isn't one of those "you're not macho if you can't take a few sharks in your face" things; the boat only goes out when there are people who really want to dive with the sharks. But for those who do, it's not something they're likely to forget soon.

There are other places where you can dive with sharks; there are places where they'll take you out to a reef, back you up to a coral head, and then bait in a couple of sharks.

Here, there is no reef. You're floating in clear blue water that measures two miles on the vertical. And since sharks rarely attend a party unless they're invited, the crew chums the water a bit to let the sharks know its showtime. Then they come in—little three-footers (1 meter) right on up to six- to eight-foot models (3-4 meters). The dive-masters feed the sharks ballyhoo, and you can get as close to the action as you want. To us, this seems a bit like sitting in the front row to watch a fire-breather, but there are a lot of takers.

The dive is as safe as this sort of thing can be. Cove says he's been to the buoy dozens of times in the past few years and has brought hundreds of divers to see the sharks without any untoward incidents (i.e., no missing limbs). The silky sharks seem to be able to distinguish between the bait and the divers pretty well.

Sharks, of course, are always unpredictable, and if you have any notion that seeing an eating machine the size of an oil drum headed for your face mask would upset you, check out the video before you sign up for the dive. Nassau Undersea Adventures has some terrific video of the shark dive so you can get a preview from the comfort and safety of the dive shop before you buy your ticket.

Other operators on the island have taken up the gauntlet and also offer trips to The Buoy. Despite the increase in traffic, there still are no reports of injuries to divers and the sharks don't seem to mind the company, showing up for dinner whenever they're invited. *Goombay Magazine* (the Bahamasair in-flight publication) even published a photo by noted underwater photographer Rick Frehsee showing a bikini-clad diver holding a three-foot silky shark over her head. With all this publicity, maybe shark-pressing will become a popular form of aerobic exercise. We'd like to see Jane Fonda's next workout video top that for excitement.

Unlike most of the other dives in this book, The Buoy is an offshore dive. And unlike the other dives, the weather is a major consideration in whether or not you'll be able to dive it during your stay.

While there are always some sites around New Providence proper that are in a lee, The Buoy is totally open to whatever fronts, storms, or other disturbances are moving through. With the exception of tropical depressions, storms and fronts in the Caribbean tend to be short-lived phenomena. With no major land masses to hold them up, they tend to "blow through" quickly, lingering a day or two at the most. The weather is the most dicey in December and January when strong high-pressure fronts from North America sometimes make it to the Bahamas before dissipating. Most other months, the usual tropical calm prevails. If you really want to do The Buoy, plan to stay a week. That should give you an ample weather window.

Despite the raft of movies showing sharks chasing down divers, at The Buoy you'll get a better feel for reality: Divers chasing sharks. Photo: S. Cove

Typical depth range	:	10-20 ft. (3-6 m)
Typical current conditions	:	none
Expertise required	:	novice
Access	:	boat

The LCT wreck is a World War II-vintage LST that was used to ferry freight back and forth to Exuma in the years after the war. While making its way out of Nassau Harbour, it began taking on water. The crew ran it aground to try to salvage the cargo, and it settled into its present position, just on the southwest side of Athol Island.

The water over the top of the wheelhouse is only knee deep, and it's about 20 feet (6 meters) to the sand. The boat is fairly intact.

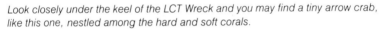

Look closely under the keel of the LCT Wreck and you may find a tiny arrow crab, like this one, nestled among the hard and soft corals.

A piece of the wreckage, perhaps part of the engine, lies a few yards behind the LCT wreck. The metal is liberally coated with encrusting sponge and soft corals. Small tropicals may be found inside.

Although LSTs are not the most exciting wrecks to look at, this one is fun, partly because of the sea fans and rope sponges rooted to its decks, and the presence of large fish.

The decks and doorways are pretty well coated with fire coral, so wear a wetsuit or be careful.

The forward cabin is pretty open, and there's a cable coiled up on the floor. With the light flooding in through gaping holes in the sides and top, it makes a nice photo with a strobe or with available light. The north side of the wreck has a knob of brain coral the size of a bowling ball growing on one of the gunwales. Try getting in close to this with a wide-angle lens and light it with your strobe.

Behind and to the south of the wreck is a large, square, boxlike affair. With a wide angle lens, this will fill the front of your film frame, and the wreck can be seen in the background.

Look in the sand underneath the stern. You may find any assortment of large or small tropicals hiding in the sponge, algae and coral piled up in the shadows where the prop used to be.

Typical depth range	:	45 ft. (14 m)
Typical current conditions	:	light
Expertise required	:	intermediate
Access	:	boat

The caves are due north of the Club Med beach on Paradise Island. The name is misleading; actually there is a quintet of grottoes, not a trio. In addition to the three main caves, there are two smaller ones a few hundred feet to the west.

Large groupers are very common in the area of Trinity Caves. Though the area lacks abundant hard coral, soft corals are plentiful, and the cave walls are covered with encrusting growth. Photo.

A coney, hovering just in front of the fantastic variegated background of Trinity Caves, is caught in the middle of a color change. Like a chameleon lizard on land, these groupers can change their colors at will to better blend with their environment.

The reef here is mostly limestone, with abundant soft corals—gorgonians and sea fans—but little hard coral. There's a large stand of rare pillar coral, though. Tube worms cover the surface of the rocks, which is carpeted with calcareous algae.

This site might be called the Spiny Lobster Sheraton; the crevices and small holes in the limestone substrate are literally crawling with lobsters. However, this is definitely not the place to dive for dinner. Trinity Caves is part of the area protected from hunting and collecting of any sort.

The caves are coated with a thick lining of sponges and other encrusting growth. Clusters of purple and brown tube sponges, green rope sponges, and whip corals dangle from the walls and ceilings.

Big animals are often spotted near the caves. Large groupers are seen often, and rays with 6-foot wingspans aren't uncommon.

Typical depth range	:	45 ft. (14 m)
Typical current conditions	:	moderate to heavy
Expertise required	:	intermediate
Access	:	boat

The *Mahoney* is something of a mystery. Interestingly, the boat's name was never *Mahoney,* and no one seems to know why it's called that now. The ship was a 212-foot (64 meter) steel freighter that went down in the hurricane of 1929. It broke in two while sinking, and the stern and the bow are now about 100 yards (90 meters) apart.

The wreck was dynamited flat to prevent other ships from hitting it, so there isn't a great deal of relief to the wreck.

When dive guides start their fish feeding routine, the first animals in are often enormous horse-eyed jacks. These big, bullish-looking fish are fast, strong, and aggressive.

Though it was blasted flat so as not to interfere with shipping, the Mahoney *can still be recognized beneath the encrusting growth.*

The steam boiler, located off to the southwest side of the main wreckage, was left intact. It's heavily encrusted with fire coral (watch those ungloved hands) and is a marvelous photographic prop.

The fish here are photogenic as well. They're accustomed to being fed, and are a little tamer than at many other sites around the island.

The substrate around the *Mahoney* is littered with gorgonians and other soft corals.

Normally, the operators only dive the *Mahoney* at slack tide, as there's a fast current over the wreck when the tide is moving, and especially on a falling tide.

Typical depth range	:	25 ft. (8 m)
Typical current conditions	:	light
Expertise required	:	novice
Access	:	boat

You've doubtless already seen this reef—this is where the speargun sequence in *Thunderball* was filmed. It's worth seeing in person, though. The area is a large patch-reef complex with numerous brain and star coral heads. The reef is long and narrow, and runs north and south, perpendicular to New Providence.

Located just off Athol Island, the Thunderball Reef was the area used to film part of the James Bond movie of the same name. Photo: H. Taylor.

Thunderball is one of the more scenic shallow reef areas around New Providence. A tangle of elkhorn growth provides shelter for numerous small tropicals and even a few lobsters. As the reef is located inside of the Bahamas Marine Park, no lobsters may be taken from the area. Photo: H. Taylor.

The whole reef takes in an area about 100 yards by 35 yards (90 meters by 30 meters). The tops of the coral heads come to within 10 feet (3 meters) of the surface, making it an excellent snorkeling area as well. Hordes of small tropicals crowd the undercuts at the base of the heads, and lobsters can be seen at night.

The shallow bottom, abundant light reflecting off the sand, and fishlife make this a good place to get in some macrophotography. If you look carefully into the crevices and around the edges of the sponges you may see tiny, translucent ghost shrimp, barely large enough to fill a 1:1 macro framer.

Typical depth range	:	100 ft. (30 m)
Typical current conditions	:	light
Expertise required	:	intermediate to expert
Access	:	boat

Wrecking, or salvaging goods from vessels run up on shallow reefs, was the first major industry in the Bahamas. There are stories that the old-time Bahamian wreckers were not exactly averse to moving warning lights around to make navigation in the shoal-strewn waters around New Providence even chancier. Although the business died out in the 19th century, it seems to be making a comeback of sorts with the advent of scuba diving. The stakes aren't quite as serious, as the "victims" are all derelict vessels and all that's salvaged are good times and photographs. Today's wreckers are the dive operators, who have deliberately put down some of the finest wrecks in the Caribbean. The *Never Say Never Again* wreck on the south side is one. The *Alcora* is another.

This 130-foot (40 m) ship was confiscated by the Bahamas government and turned over to Sun Divers for disposal. The only proviso was that they sink the hull in a place where it wouldn't be a hazard to navigation.

Once used by drug smugglers the Alcora *now carries a cargo of marine life. The vessel was cleaned and stripped of hatches and glass, and deliberately sunk. Photo: H. Taylor.*

There's very little danger of that—it's 80 feet (25 meters) to the deck. Even though the wreck is deep, it's gorgeous. The boat is sitting upright on a sand bottom, surrounded by low, mounding corals.

The ports are open and you can swim through the two large cargo holds in the forward and middle portions of the ship. A light will be needed to penetrate the engine room.

The water over the wreck is often a little murky so, descending through it, you'll at first see nothing but gauzy blue. As you go deeper, the indistinct outlines of the ship begin to form a huge shadow lurking below. Like an amusement park ride, it's a little spooky until the water clears just above the wreck and the entire hull, sitting clean and upright, can be seen.

The operators generally run to the *Alcora* when they have a large enough group of experienced divers to make up a trip. It may be worth mentioning your interest in seeing the wreck early on in your stay, so the operators can more easily find a group qualified to make the dive.

French angelfish are among the dozens of species that inhabit the Alcora *wreck. Since its hatches, doors, and glass were removed before it was sunk, the ship is very safe for divers, making it one of the premiere wreck dives in the Caribbean.*

Typical depth range	:	10 ft. (3 m)
Typical current conditions	:	light
Expertise required	:	novice
Access	:	boat or beach

Balmoral Island isn't on any dive operator's regular schedule, but it could make a nice outing if you decide to take an afternoon off to snorkel. Particularly for novice snorkelers and children, the area is a terrific introduction to the joys of mask and flippers.

The island is located at the mouth of Goodman's Bay, directly north of the Cable Beach Hotel at Cable Beach.

Balmoral is part of a line of barrier islands that run along the outer reef line of the north shore of New Providence. As such, it has a seaward side and a "lagoon" side. Even when the ocean is a bit rough, there's usually a lee to get away from the swells. The only exception is when the wind blows east to west, sending swells down both sides of the island.

Balmoral Island is part of a chain of barrier islands that run along the outer reef line of the north shore of New Providence. The reef can be clearly seen as the line where the dark blue deep water meets the turquoise of the shallows.

The crystalline, shallow waters of Balmoral Island make a delightful afternoon diversion for snorkelers. Small tropicals, such as this pufferfish, are common on the north side of the island. Particularly for children, it's a good idea to outfit everyone with work gloves. Though you may have trouble finding child-sized gloves, even the overly-large adult sizes are good protection against spines and fire coral. Photo: H. Taylor.

Balmoral is a fair distance from shore, so the best bet is to find a ski boat willing to drop you off and pick you up, or a small boat you can rent for the afternoon. Pull up on the south side, facing shore, and walk across to the ocean side.

The reef line, just offshore, is primarily rocky limestone substrate, with little live coral development. The rocks at the back of the reef harbor an incredible aquarium of small tropicals representing the whole range of Caribbean species.

Bring a lunch and enjoy the privacy. Very few of Nassau's million tourists ever make it to this beautiful little bit of the tropics.

4

Dangerous Marine Life

There aren't many things to worry about while diving around New Providence. The standard Caribbean cautions apply, but even the ubiquitous sea urchins that bedevil the shallow diving of many islands are in short supply here.

Sea urchins. These little long-spined guys look like elaborate pincushions. An essential part of the reef community, urchins graze on algae. They help keep coral healthy by removing algae growths that may settle on a coral's surface and prevent it from feeding.

Backing into or sitting on an urchin may result in the spines puncturing your skin, then breaking off inside. Usually, the reaction is no more than a rash and a little swelling, although some people are more sensitive to spines. After a few days, the spines will dissolve. If they're very bothersome, you might try digging them out with a needle as you would a wood splinter.

Playing with a stonefish is an absolute no-no. The diver here is taking a great risk. The venom contained in the spines of stonefish can cause serious injury or even death.

Fire coral. The most common danger is also the easiest to avoid. Fire coral is not true coral, it's actually a relative of the jellyfish. Fire coral grows over the skeleton of sea fans, encrusts metal objects, and sometimes grows into sheetlike blades standing upright from the bottom. When something, like an unprotected hand, brushes fire coral, small stinging cells called nematocysts inject an irritating chemical into the skin. The resulting rash and burning sensation may last a couple of days.

Most problems with fire coral involve divers backing into it or sitting down on it accidentally. The LCT wreck, for example, is generously coated with fire coral. If you are stung, try rubbing a hydrocortisone first aid cream on the rash, or put some meat tenderizer on it.

Stonefish. Stonefish are members of the scorpionfish family. Aptly named, they look like lumps of algae-covered rock. Generally they just lie on the bottom, so when settling down, check to see that the rocks around you are, in fact, rocks. The spines just forward of the stonefish's dorsal fin can inject a powerful poison if they puncture the skin.

Fire coral may look like a regular coral colony, or it may be found as an encrusting growth on a wreck, on rocks, or even on sea fans. Wherever you find it, keep your distance. The rash it causes isn't serious, but it is annoying. Photo: H. Taylor.

Moray eels. There are some gigantic green morays hiding in the reefs around New Providence. Like most other things in the sea, they aren't really dangerous unless you insist on harassing them. It's a good idea to keep your hands out of dark crevices under the reef. You may stick your hand in a hole and pull it back with an eel attached to it. If you do see an eel, it won't hurt to examine it from a respectful distance, but if the eel decides to retreat, it's best to let it go.

Sharks. Sharks are everywhere. However, some places have fewer sharks than others, and New Providence is one of these. You're not likely to see anything but nurse sharks in the shallows of the north side or south side. There are some pelagic sharks, such as hammerheads, on the more isolated sections of the south side. Spearing fish with scuba is against the law here anyway, so divers have little to fear from any stray sharks they may encounter.

Rays. There are a fair number of rays around New Providence. Rays, once called "devilfish" by sailors, are not really devilish at all. Like stonefish, they mostly lie on the bottom minding their own business. However, they don't care to be stepped on, sat on, or prodded. The sharp barb near the base of the tail can inflict a very deep and painful wound. One diver who accidentally stepped on a ray and was hit in the leg likened it to getting shot with a .22 caliber rifle.

Bristle worms are also called fire worms. Like fire coral, brushing against one could result in a burning sensation, usually followed by a slight rash. The best treatment is hydrocortisone cream. Photo: H. Taylor.

The small lump at the base of this stingray's tail is the stinger. Rays are very docile and are only dangerous if they're kicked, prodded, or sat on. As this ray demonstrates, the animals are sometimes hard to distinguish from the scrabble of a patch reef.

5

Safety

The diving operators on New Providence are conscientious about their customers. They'll be more than happy to assist you in any way to make your diving safer and more fun. Ultimately, however, your personal safety is your responsibility. Listen closely to dive guides and instructors, and follow their directions. Also be aware of what your options are or aren't during each dive. If you don't remember how to use the dive tables, ask for help. You'll look a whole lot less foolish getting help with the tables before a dive than you will having to ask for emergency help afterwards.

Chambers. Information on chambers is offered here only as a convenience. Because the status and location of hyperbaric chambers changes, we can't be responsible for the accuracy of information. Get the information you need *before* leaving the U.S., and write it in a place that's accessible, such as in your dive log.

The closest emergency chamber is in Grand Bahama. The closest full-service chamber is in Miami, an hour's flight away. In case of an accident, there are two places you can call. The first is the Bahamas Air Sea Rescue, or BASRA. Their number is 809-322-3877 or 325-3743. The second is the Diver's Alert Network.

DAN, the **Diver's Alert Network,** operates a **24-hour national hotline, (919) 684-8111** (collect calls are accepted in an emergency). DAN does not provide medical care, although they do provide advice on early treatment, evacuation, and hyperbaric treatment. Divers should not call DAN for chamber locations in advance of an accident as chamber status changes frequently. Instead, divers should contact DAN as soon as a diving emergency is suspected. DAN can give advice on the nearest facility able to handle the emergency. All divers should have comprehensive medical insurance and make sure that hyperbaric treatment and air ambulance services are covered.

Originally federally funded, DAN is now largely supported by the diving public. Membership is $10 a year and all donations are tax deductible as DAN is a chartered non-profit organization. Membership includes the DAN *Underwater Diving Accident Manual*, a card giving DAN's phone numbers, decals listing the emergency number, and other benefits. Contact DAN by writing: Administrative Coordinator, National Diving Alert Network, Duke University Medical Center, P.O. Box 3823, Durham, NC 27710, or call the DAN office at (919) 684-2948.

Appendix—

Diving Operators of New Providence

At the time of publication, this list was current, but new dive operations may open or established operators may change names, locations or telephone numbers. This list is provided as a service to the reader and does not constitute an endorsement of the operators and dive shops. If you have questions about the names and locations, the Bahamas Ministry of Tourism office in Miami is always a good source of information. They can be reached at (305) 442-4869 or by writing: Bahamas Ministry of Tourism, 255 Alhambra Circle, Coral Gables, FL 33134.

Bahamas Divers
P.O. Box 5004
Nassau, Bahamas
(809) 393-3431

Dive Dive Dive, Ltd.
Box N8050,
Nassau, Bahamas
(809) 362-1401 or (809) 362-1143
In the U.S.: (800) 328-8029 ext. 246

Nassau Undersea Adventures
P.O. Box CB 11697
Nassau, Bahamas
In the U.S.: (800) 468-9876 or (305) 359-3066 (Aero International Tours)
In New Providence: (809) 362-4171

Peter Hughes Dive South Ocean
Divi Resorts
54 Gunderman Rd.
Ithaca, NY 14850
In the U.S.: (800) 333-3484 (Divi Resorts Reservation Line)
In New Providence: (809) 362-4391

Sun Divers
P.O. Box N10728
Nassau, Bahamas
(809) 325-8927

Index